Market-Fresh

Market-Fresh Mixology

Cocktails for Every Season

Bridget Albert WITH Mary Barranco

SURREY
BOOKS

CHICAGO

Cocktail photographs copyright 2008 by Tim Turner. Author photographs by Larry Fox.

Book design and layout: Brandtner Design

Printed in China.

Library of Congress Cataloging-in-Publication Data

Albert, Bridget.
 Market-fresh mixology : cocktails for every season / Bridget Albert with Mary Barranco.
    p. cm.
 Includes index.
 ISBN-13: 978-1-57284-095-9 (hardcover)
 ISBN-10: 1-57284-095-1 (hardcover)
 1. Cocktails. I. Barranco, Mary. II. Title.
 TX951.A33 2008
 641.8'74–dc22
                          2008009547

10 9 8 7 6 5 4 3 2

Surrey Books is an imprint of Agate Publishing. Agate books are available in bulk at discount prices. For more information, go to agatepublishing.com.

We dedicate this book to our children, Paige, Allison, and Michael.

Table of Contents

Acknowledgments

A special thank you from my heart to my husband, Jamie; our daughter, Paige; my brother, Brian; my sister-in-law, Kasia; my parents, Nancy and David; and my Grandma Rosella. Thank you for your words of encouragement. Thank you, also, to my in-laws, aunts, uncles, cousins, and friends, who were the finest taste-testers. Finally, a warm thank you to my mentor, teacher, and friend, Tony Abou-Ganim.

Cheers,
Bridget

Thanks to my wonderful family, especially my husband, Joe; our children, Michael and Allison; my sisters, Teresa and Cathy, who are also my best friends and constant source of courage; and, last but not least, my brother Peter, who can fix anything.

Mary

We both extend gratitude to our work family and employer, Southern Wine & Spirits of Illinois, and our general manager, Will Conniff, who provides the format for us to bring our passion to the trade.

We also extend a special thank you to the members of the United States Bartenders Guild, for their dedication and drive in raising the bar.

"Fresh fruit is not enough. Finding local fruit that is picked off the tree when it is ripe is superior. It provides better taste that explodes in a subtle way. This means finding a local farm you trust. The winter is a challenge... we have to rely on the in-season fruits we get from California and Florida... "

Bob Pallotta
Slow Food Chairman

"Farmers welcome each season. We look forward to planting in the spring, summer growth, and fall harvest. Winter is a time for us to rest and reflect on the year before. We look to Mother Nature to provide everything else."

Farmer John Thompson
Morris, Illinois

Introduction

Whether you are entertaining a large crowd, hosting a cocktail party, or spending the evening with a close friend, a cocktail is meant to be savored.

Like fine wines, a memorable cocktail needs layers of flavor. **My only rule is that cocktails must be balanced with freshness**. This book will show you each step in making these simple, fresh, and modern cocktails, as you learn to enhance the classics. Great classics, such as the Mojito, which emerged in the mid 1900s, are making the scene again for your sipping pleasure. One of my favorite twists on this classic, the Blueberry Lavender Mojito, adds a splash of culinary freshness and creativity.

All great recipes require the basics. Up front, you'll find a section on *Home Bar Essentials,* which gives you the fundamentals of cocktail creation with a quick reference outlining the right spirits, store-bought and homemade mixers, tools, and glassware needed to complete each cocktail. As you read on in the book, you'll see that each recipe includes an easy-to-follow format with a *Tool Box* of supplies for every recipe.

The changing seasons are the inspiration for every recipe in *Market-Fresh Mixology,* including the spring-fresh Rhubarb Strawberry

Collins and the winter-savory Caviar Martini. These recipes feature your favorite spirits, like vodka, tequila, gin, bourbon, or sparkling wine for celebration cocktails, mixed with delicious ingredients from each chapter's *Season's Best* list of flavorful in-season produce.

In the final chapter, you'll learn the art of making cocktail infusions, such as Bing Cherries with Cinnamon and Bourbon. Infusions capture the spirits and flavors of the season as they meld together over time.

As you read through, enjoy the tidbits of cocktail lore and historic drinking toasts. I'm sure they will inspire you to make the freshest cocktails the season has to offer. Let's raise the bar as we raise our glasses. Cheers!

Home Bar Essentials

TOOLS OF THE TRADE

Just like an artist needs a paintbrush, paint, and a canvas, there are a few basic tools for the home bartender. Making consistently great cocktails requires the freshest ingredients and key essentials, such as the shaker, strainer, muddler, and bar spoon. Like most home goods, these tools are, depending on the quality, available for a wide range of prices. The next few pages outline some bar-tool necessities.

Shakers

There are two basic styles to choose from.

Boston shaker: A two-piece shaker consisting of a tin and a pint glass. A separate strainer is required. The Boston shaker is most often selected by classic bartenders and is a personal favorite.

Cobbler: A three-piece metal cocktail shaker with a built-in strainer and a cap.

Strainers

Hawthorn strainer: A metal strainer designed to fit over the top of a cocktail shaker to strain the drink into the glass. Has 2-4 prongs, and a spring around the outer edge that fits over the cocktail shaker. Controls the speed of the pour while keeping ice in the shaker.

Julep strainer: A strainer that is placed over the glass of a Boston shaker to remove ice and strain the cocktail. Similar in appearance to a slotted spoon and most often used for bourbon cocktails that are traditionally stirred in the pint glass of a shaker.

Other Tools

Bar spoon: A long spoon with a twisted handle used to stir cocktails directly in a serving glass or the pint glass of the Boston shaker.

Muddler: A small club used to crush, mash, or grind ingredients in order to release essential flavors and oils. The muddler is placed directly in the cocktail or pint glass, and it is used with motions similar to those used with a mortar and pestle.

Citrus press: A hand-held juicer designed to extract juice from citrus fruit.

Citrus peeler: A thin, sharp tool used to separate a citrus fruit's peel from its pith. [Most often used for making garnishes.]

Jigger: A double-sided liquid measuring tool with a jigger (which measures 1½ ounces) on one side and a pony (which measures 1 ounce) on the reverse side.

Zester/grater: A utensil with sharp raised areas that is used to grate small pieces of fruit or spices.

Corkscrew: An apparatus with a handle and a sharp metal spiral that is used to remove corks from wine bottles. A waiter's corkscrew also has a small blade to cut the foil on a wine bottle.

Bottle opener: A device used to remove the caps from some beer and soda bottles

Sieve: A metal utensil made of mesh that is used to separate particles from liquid. Traditionally, a bartender-size sieve is 2-3 inches in diameter.

Paring knife: A short-bladed knife used to peel and slice fruit and vegetables.

Cutting board: A small, washable surface will suffice for most bars.

Other necessities include:

Bar towel

Ice bucket and scoop

Cocktail napkins

Cocktail picks

Glassware Suggestions

One of the most often-asked questions about cocktails and home bartending is not only what to serve, but how best to serve it. Every well-stocked bar should have the appropriate glassware for cocktail, wine, and beer service. Your choices in glassware style and costs are unlimited. Once you have the basics, as outlined here, you can continue to add interesting specialty glasses, including brandy snifters, cordial glasses, and fun collectibles.

The next question you need to consider is the quantity to purchase. Analyze your entertainment style. Do you host large events with many guests, or are you more likely to have cozy gatherings? At minimum, have six of each of these basics on hand, and select styles that have been in production for some time and are likely to continue to be available, so you can add more later if necessary.

Cocktail glass   *Tall/Collins glass*   *Rocks glass*   *White wine glass*

Red wine glass   *Champagne flute*   *Pint glass for beer*

Spirits, Wine, and Beer

Having a well-stocked bar insures guest satisfaction, no matter the request. The Home Bar Essentials *Spirit List* gives basic product suggestions and descriptions. Be sure to have on hand at least one selection in each spirit category. Later, add items like mezcal or rye whiskey to create variety and enhance the flavors of your crafted cocktails. Customize your bar by adding neighborhood favorites like beer from local breweries.

SPIRIT LIST

Vodka: A neutral spirit without a distinctive taste, aroma, character, or color. Flavored vodkas can enhance cocktails, and many enjoy citrus-flavored vodkas in particular.

Gin: A distilled spirit, with its main flavors coming from juniper and other botanicals.

Rum: A spirit made from sugarcane, sugarcane syrup, or molasses that can be matured and blended. White and dark rum are the bar basics. Other styles include:

- Golden
- Añejo, Vieux, age-dated
- Spiced, flavored

Tequila: A distinctive product of Mexico that is derived principally from the agave tequilana weber ("blue" variety). The following styles are widely available.

- Silver/bianco (unaged)
- Reposado (aged for at least 2 months)
- Añejo (aged for up to 12 months)

A silver tequila is unaged and therefore has a simple flavor. It is a blank canvas suitable for most margaritas. Match the bold flavors of aged tequilas with heartier fruits and cocktails.

Scotch whisky: A product of Scotland, manufactured in compliance with the laws of the United Kingdom. If it is a mixture of whiskies, it's labeled a "blended Scotch whisky." A single-malt Scotch comes from a single distillery in Scotland and is made from or of malted barley. Best consumed straight up or on the rocks.

One blended Scotch and one single-malt from the Highlands will suffice as you begin to build your bar inventory. Explore regions like Islay and the Lowlands as you expand into a wider style and taste variety in single-malts.

Whiskey, whisky, and bourbon: All a basic bar needs is one favorite bourbon and one favorite rye whiskey. Experiment with variety and other selections over time.

- American whiskey: This whiskey is made in the United States from a grain mash and aged in oak.

- Bourbon whiskey: Bourbon is produced only in the United States and made from 51% corn mash and Kentucky spring water. If it is less than 4 years old, its age must be displayed on the bottle.

- Canadian whisky: Canadian whisky (note that it does not include the "e" in the spelling) derives from a mash of various grains and is aged in oak for three years.

- Corn whiskey: At least 80% of this whiskey's mash is corn.

- Rye whiskey: This whiskey is predominantly rye mash and is aged at least 2 years in charred oak barrels.

- Tennessee whiskey: Made only in Tennessee, this whiskey is filtered through sugar-maple charcoal and aged for 2 years in new charred barrels.

Brandy/cognac: Brandy is a distilled spirit made from the juice of fruit or grapes, and cognac is a type of brandy made from grapes grown under strict regulations in the Cognac region of France. Some common and unofficial brandy grades include:

- VS (very special): Aged at least 2.5 years in casks
- VSOP (very superior old pale): Aged a minimum of 4.5 years in casks.
- XO (extra old): Aged at least 6.5 years in casks.

Flavored liqueurs: These liqueurs are made by mixing or redistilling spirits over fruits or botanicals through infusion, percolation, or maceration. Some common favorites are:

- Amaretto
- Anisette
- Apricot
- Coffee
- Crème de cacao
- Crème de cassis
- Limoncello
- Maraschino
- Pomegranate
- Sloe gin
- Triple sec

Bitters: Bitters are modifiers generally made from alcohol, herbs, plants, or roots. A few drops add a great deal of flavor. The following varieties are commonly available:

- Peach
- Orange
- Blood orange
- Angostura

- Peychauds
- Mint
- Lemon
- Aged

WINES AND BEERS

Wines: Every bar should have a few bottles of the three primary varieties:
- White
- Red
- Port
- Sparkling/champagne

Beer: In order to satisfy a range of tastes, have on hand both an ale (smooth, light) and a lager (hearty, rich). The two primary types of beer are ale and lager.

- Ale is a sweet, full-bodied, and fruity beer made with top-fermenting yeast. Predominantly British and Belgian in origin. Stout is a dark ale made with roasted malt or barley that is usually fuller in flavor. Porter is sometimes used as an alternate name for stout, and it may indicate a stout that is stronger than usual. India pale ale (IPA) is a sparkling ale with a higher level of hops and a bitter flavor. Hefeweizen is an unfiltered wheat ale with a light, crisp, and fruity flavor. It is often served with a slice of lemon or orange to enhance its flavors.
- Lager is German and Czech in origin, with a wide range of flavors. Bock is a strong lager (originally from Einbeck, Germany) that may be dark, amber, or pale in color. Dopplebock is a Bavarian specialty beer that is very rich, with a malty flavor and a higher alcohol content. A pilsner is a pale lager with a light, clear-to-golden-yellow color and a distinct hoppy aroma and flavor.

Store-Bought Ingredients

Juice

- Cranberry
- Lemon
- Lime
- Grapefruit
- Orange
- Pineapple
- Tomato

Mixers

- Bottled water
- Club soda
- Cola and diet cola
- Ginger ale
- Grenadine
- Half & half
- Lemon-lime soda
- Tonic water

Standard Garnishes

- Maraschino and brandied cherries
- Spanish olives
- Lemons
- Limes
- Oranges
- Pearl onions

Homemade Ingredients

SYRUPS

Simple syrup: Simple syrup is used as a sweetening ingredient in many cocktails and is a combination of one part sugar to one part water. The basic recipe is:

Simple Syrup
- 1 cup super fine sugar
- 1 cup hot water

Stir or shake until sugar dissolves. Store in a sterile container in the refrigerator. Glass jars with lids are the preferred storage container; they are easily sterilized by filling them with boiling water.

Flavored syrups: Flavored syrups are easy to make and can enhance the classics with savory herbs and sweetness. Some syrups require adjusting the one-to-one ratio of sugar to water, but you can make almost any flavored syrup by adding your favorite flavor to the basic simple syrup recipe and following the directions below.

Brown Sugar Syrup
- 1 cup brown sugar
- 1 cup water

Cinnamon Syrup
- 1 cup super fine sugar
- 1 cup water
- 4 cinnamon sticks (or one heaping bar spoon of ground cinnamon)

Honey Syrup
- 1 cup honey
- ½ cup water

Honey Rosemary Syrup

  1 cup honey
  ½ cup water
  4 rosemary sprigs

Lavender Syrup

  ¼ cup organic dried lavender
  ½ cup super fine sugar
  1 cup water

Lemon Grass Syrup

  1 cup super fine sugar
  1 cup water
  1 lemon grass stalk (peeled and cut to fit into pan)

Vanilla Syrup

  1 cup super fine sugar
  1 cup water
  1 vanilla bean (split in half)

Bring all ingredients to a boil on medium heat. Reduce heat and simmer for 8-10 minutes, until sugar is dissolved. Stir occasionally. Let cool. Use a sieve to strain the syrup into a sterilized and sealed container. Store in the refrigerator.

SOUR MIXERS

Fresh Sour

  2 cups Fresh Lemon Juice (approximately 8 lemons juiced)
  1 cup Simple Syrup (see page 25)

Stir well. Cover. Store in the refrigerator.

Fresh Limeade

> 2 cups Fresh Lime Juice (approximately 8 limes juiced)
> 1 cup Simple Syrup (see page 25)

Stir well. Cover. Store in the refrigerator.

Adds tartness when used as an alternative to lemonade.

PURÉES

All flavors of fruit or vegetable purée can be made by following these easy directions. For fruit, simply peel and cube; for vegetables, cut and steam them. Add ingredients to a food processor or blender and blend them until smooth. For additional sweetness, add simple syrup to taste. Strain through a sieve into a sealed container. Store in the refrigerator.

ORANGE OR LEMON SPIRALS

To make a simple and beautiful garnish, use a firm, room-temperature orange or lemon and a citrus peeler. Cut the top and bottom off the citrus fruit and insert the tip of the citrus peeler in to the pith of the fruit (the white area between the peel and pulp). Without moving the tool, slowly rotate the fruit around peeler until the tip is at the midway point. Repeat from the bottom. The fruit should be completely loosened from the skin. Place a diagonal cut in the peel and remove it. All fruit and pulp should be removed from the peel. Roll the peel tightly and place a toothpick through the center to hold it in place. Cut ¼-inch slices from the rolled up fruit. Place spiral on cocktail by holding both ends of the spiral and gently twisting and spreading it open in one quick motion.

Spring

Rebirth. Renewal. Anticipation.

Carrot Chic

A fresh welcome to spring.

TOOL BOX

► Mixing glass
► Tin
► Strainer
► Bar spoon
► Knife
► Electric juicer

Cocktail glass

1½ ounce carrot juice (about 2 medium carrots)
½ ounce Fresh Sour (see page 26)
1½ ounces orange vodka
½ ounce triple sec
Baby carrot (for garnish)

RIM INGREDIENTS
3 bar spoons super fine sugar
½ bar spoon ground ginger
Lime wedge

TO RIM THE GLASS:

Measure sugar and ginger onto a small plate. Stir. Rim the outside top of glass with lime wedge. Roll the outside lip of glass in sugar mixture. Set aside.

Add carrot juice, Fresh Sour, orange vodka, and triple sec to mixing glass. Add ice to your tin. Shake well. Strain into cocktail glass.

Garnish with a baby carrot.

TOOL BOX

▸ Mixing glass
▸ Tin
▸ Strainer
▸ Muddler
▸ Knife

Rocks glass

Cucumber Caipiroska

A refreshing spa experience in a glass.

4 lime wedges
1 ounce Simple Syrup (see page 25)
2 cucumber wheels (½-inch)
1½ ounces pear vodka

To a short glass, add lime wedges, Simple Syrup, cucumbers and vodka. Muddle until ingredients are combined well. Add ice to tin. Pour ingredients from short glass to mixing glass. Reserve the short glass. Shake well. Dump all ingredients from the shaker back into the seasoned short glass, and serve.

The Caipirinha and Caipiroska are the only classic cocktails muddled, shaken, and poured without straining into a serving glass. Made with a Brazilian rum called cachaca, which is made of 100% sugar cane, the Caipirinha was originally known as a "peasant drink" and is the national drink of Brazil. The Caipiroska is a vodka-based variation of the drink that is more popular among young Brazilian adults.

Rhubarb Strawberry Collins

A sweet and juicy addition to the classic Collins.

5 large, ripe strawberries

1 stalk of rhubarb

1½ ounces Fresh Sour (see page 26)

1½ ounces gin

Splash of pasteurized egg white (look for small cartons of pasteurized
   egg white in the dairy section)

Club soda

In electric juicer, juice 4 strawberries, set aside. Juice rhubarb into a separate dish. Set aside.

To mixing glass, add 1 ounce strawberry juice, 1½ ounces rhubarb juice, Fresh Sour, gin, and the splash of egg white. Add ice to tin and tall glass. Shake well. Strain into the iced-filled glass. Top with club soda.

Garnish with a strawberry heart by slicing strawberry lengthwise into thin slices.

This drink dates from the late 1800s. Cocktail lore suggests this recipe is inspired by the Collins, which may have been invented in St. Louis or London. One story suggests that the original Tom Collins was made with "Old Tom" gin, a sweetened variety of gin that was available before London dry gin. When made with gin and Fresh Sour, the Collins is a true classic.

Spring Fresco

Perfect for an outdoor cocktail party.

TOOL BOX

- ▶ Mixing glass
- ▶ Tin
- ▶ Strainer
- ▶ Muddler
- ▶ Knife

Cocktail glass

10 tarragon leaves

4 thin radish slices

4 thin cucumber slices

½ ounce bianco vermouth

1 ounce grapefruit vodka

½ ounce Fresh Sour (see page 26)

½ ounce fresh orange juice

1 radish and tarragon sprig (for garnish)

In mixing glass, muddle tarragon, radish and cucumber slices, and vermouth. Add vodka, Fresh Sour, and orange juice. Add ice to tin. Shake well. Strain into cocktail glass.

Garnish with a radish wheel and tarragon sprig.

The Green Mule

TOOL BOX

▶ Bar spoon
▶ Knife
▶ Muddler

Rocks glass

A fresh twist on the classic Moscow Mule.

3 zucchini wheels
1 cucumber wheel
Juice of 1 lime wedge
2 ounces vodka
4 ounces ginger beer
Zucchini stick (for garnish)

In short glass, muddle zucchini, cucumber, and juice squeezed from lime wedge. Add vodka. Fill glass with crushed ice and top with ginger beer. Stir well. Garnish with a zucchini stick.

Fresh Strawberry Daiquiri

A traditional Daiquiri with a kiss of spring.

TOOL BOX

- Mixing glass
- Tin
- Strainer
- Muddler
- Bar spoon
- Citrus press
- Knife

Cocktail glass

2 sliced strawberries (optional)
½ ounce orange liqueur (optional)
1½ ounces white rum
1 bar spoon super fine sugar
Juice of ½ a pressed lime
Whole strawberry (for garnish)

RIM INGREDIENTS
4 bar spoons super fine sugar
Lime wedge

TO RIM THE GLASS:

Measure sugar onto a small plate. Rim the outside top of glass with the lime wedge. Roll the outside lip of the glass in sugar. Set aside.

In mixing glass, muddle strawberry slices and orange liqueur. Add rum, sugar, and lime. Add ice to tin. Shake well. Strain into sugar-rimmed glass.

Garnish with a strawberry.

The Daiquiri's main ingredients are rum, lime juice, and sugar. Jennings Cox, an American mining engineer working in Cuba for the Spanish American Iron Company, invented this drink in 1905 at the Venus Bar in Santiago, Cuba. It was a favorite of John F. Kennedy and Ernest Hemingway, who popularized the Daiquiri in the United States.

Spiced Beet Cocktail

A sophisticated, balanced blend of bold, spicy flavors.

TOOL BOX

▸ Sauté pan
▸ Citrus press
▸ Bar spoon
▸ Mixing glass
▸ Tin
▸ Strainer
▸ Knife

Cocktail glass

1 beet (peeled and sliced)
Juice of 3 pressed limes
2 bar spoons brown sugar
Pinch of ground ginger
1½ ounces silver tequila
½ ounce mezcal
1 ounce Fresh Sour (see page 26)
1 beet leaf (for garnish)

To sauté pan, add sliced beet, lime juice, brown sugar, and ground ginger. Cover and simmer on medium heat for about 10 minutes, or until beets are tender. Stir occasionally. Remove beets. Let liquid cool.

To mixing glass, add silver tequila, mezcal, cooled beet liquid (about 2 ounces), and Fresh Sour. Add ice to tin. Shake well. Strain into cocktail glass.

Garnish with beet leaf.

Papaya Pisco Sour

Pairs wonderfully with Latin cuisine and spicy appetizers.

TOOL BOX

▶ Mixing glass
▶ Tin
▶ Strainer
▶ Muddler
▶ Knife

Cocktail glass

3 papaya cubes
Juice of 1 pressed lime
1 ounce Simple Syrup (see page 25)
2 ounces pisco brandy
Splash of pasteurized egg white (look for small cartons of pasteurized egg white in the dairy section)
Angostura bitters

Peel and cube papaya. In mixing glass, muddle papaya and lime juice. Add Simple Syrup, pisco brandy, and egg white. Add ice to tin. Shake hard. Strain into cocktail glass. Garnish with 3 drops Angostura bitters.

The Pisco Sour is the national drink of Chile and Peru, and which country the drink actually originated in is the subject of much dispute. Pisco is a brandy made from the grapes of the wine producing areas of both countries.

A Toast for Spring

Happiness is like a kiss,
It feels better when you give it to someone else.

To each, to all, happiness, health,
And fortunes grown tall.

May we be happy and our enemies know it.

Here's to happy times,
May they come often and stay long!

Summer

Blossoming. Fresh. Inspirational.

Watermelon Margarita

Brings together cocktail and picnic traditions.

TOOL BOX

▶ Mixing glass
▶ Tin
▶ Strainer
▶ Knife
▶ Muddler
▶ Bar spoon
▶ Citrus press

Cocktail glass

4 watermelon cubes (1–inch) (seeds removed)
Juice of ½ a pressed lime
1½ ounces Fresh Sour (see page 26)
1½ ounces silver tequila
½ ounce triple sec
Watermelon wedge (for garnish)

RIM INGREDIENTS
4 bar spoons super fine sugar
1 bar spoon sea salt
1 bar spoon pink peppercorns (crushed)
Lime wedge

TO RIM THE GLASS:

On a small plate, measure sugar, sea salt, and crushed pink pepper-corns. Stir gently. Rim the outside top of the glass with a lime wedge. Roll the outside lip of the glass in the sugar mixture. Set aside.

In mixing glass, muddle watermelon cubes and lime juice. Add Fresh Sour, tequila, and triple sec. Add ice to tin. Shake all ingredients well. Strain into rimmed cocktail glass. Garnish with a watermelon wedge.

The Margarita is surrounded by many stories, and no one is certain who created this cocktail. Credit could go to a Mexico City socialite named Margarita, who charged her bartender with making a signature cocktail

(CONTINUED ON NEXT PAGE)

(CONTINUED FROM PREVIOUS PAGE)

appropriate for her many parties. Another bit of lore surrounding this blend of tequila and triple sec names Pancho Morales of Tommy's Place in Juarez, Mexico, as the drink's creator. According to that story, a woman ordered a Magnolia cocktail, which is made with brandy, triple sec and champagne. Pancho could not recall the Magnolia's ingredients, so he improvised, and the Margarita was born. Whichever story is true, one thing is for sure —the Margarita is America's best-selling cocktail.

Breakfast Cocktail

A favorite addition to any brunch.

TOOL BOX

▸ Mixing glass
▸ Tin
▸ Strainer
▸ Knife
▸ Electric juicer

Tall/Collins glass

2 ounces fresh apricot juice

1 ounce fresh orange juice

2 ounces orange vodka

½ ounce pink grapefruit juice

Apricot slice (for garnish)

In an electric juicer, juice separately one ripe apricot and then one orange. Add orange vodka, apricot juice, orange juice, and pink grapefruit juice to mixing glass. Add ice to tin. Shake well. Add crushed ice to tall glass. Strain cocktail into glass.

Garnish with an apricot slice.

Tip: Remove the vodka to make a delicious alcohol-free version.

Blueberry Lavender Mojito

Lusciously aromatic with bursts of flavor.
Made to be sipped and savored.

TOOL BOX

▶ Muddler
▶ Bar spoon
▶ Citrus press
▶ Knife
▶ Straws
▶ Cocktail pick

Tall/Collins glass

10 -15 mint leaves

1 ounce Lavender Syrup (see page 26)

    [may also substitute Simple Syrup (see page 25)]

Juice of ½ a pressed lime

15 - 20 blueberries

1½ ounces white rum

Club soda

In tall glass, muddle mint leaves, Simple Syrup or Lavender Syrup, lime juice, 15 blueberries, and rum. Muddle just enough to combine flavors, being careful not to over-muddle. Fill glass with crushed ice.

Top with club soda.

Stir with bar spoon until well blended. To garnish, place 3-4 blueberries on a cocktail pick. Serve with a straw.

....

This drink dates from the early 1900s. The Mojito was created at the La Bodeguita del Medio Bar in Cuba. Ernest Hemingway made this cocktail an international sensation in the 1940s.

Peach Julep

This julep is a sure bet on Derby day.

10-15 mint leaves
1 ounce Brown Sugar Syrup (see page 25)
3 fresh peach slices
2 ounces Kentucky straight bourbon whiskey
Mint sprig (for garnish)

To a rocks glass, add mint, Brown Sugar Syrup, and peaches. Muddle until combined well. Add whiskey. Fill glass with crushed ice. Stir. Garnish with a mint sprig.

Although the Julep was created in the early 1700s, it first appeared in print in an 1803 book published in London by John Davis. Traditionally served in silver or pewter cups and held only by the bottom and top edges of the cup, it did not become the signature cocktail of Churchill Downs until 1938.

Blackberry Cinnamon Mojito

TOOL BOX

▶ Muddler
▶ Bar spoon
▶ Citrus press
▶ Knife

Tall/Collins glass

Contemporary flavors spice up the traditional Mojito.
Serve with your favorite barbecue.

10-15 mint leaves

1 ounce Cinnamon Syrup (see page 25)

    [may also substitute Simple Syrup (see page 25)]

Juice of ½ a pressed lime

8 blackberries

1½ ounces aged rum

Club soda

1 mint sprig and remaining blackberry (for garnish)

In tall glass, muddle mint, Simple or Cinnamon Syrup, lime juice, 7 blackberries, and rum. Muddle just enough to combine flavors, being careful not to over-muddle. Fill glass with crushed ice.

Top with club soda.

Stir with bar spoon until well blended. To garnish, spear a blackberry with a mint sprig.

Raspberry French 75

Toast your special occasion with a savory celebration cocktail.

TOOL BOX

- Mixing glass
- Tin
- Strainer
- Muddler

Champagne flute

4 sage leaves

5 fresh raspberries

1½ ounces Fresh Sour (see page 26)

1½ ounces gin

Splash of champagne or sparkling wine

1 sage sprig (for garnish)

In mixing glass, muddle sage leaves, 4 raspberries, and Fresh Sour. Add gin. Add ice to tin. Shake well. Add a splash of champagne to ingredients in shaker. Gently rock all ingredients. Strain into champagne glass.

Garnish with a sage sprig gently speared through remaining raspberry.

The French 75 was created by Raoul Lufbery, a pilot in the Escadrille Americaine air fighting unit. The cocktail was originally blended with cognac and champagne and was named after the World War I French artillery piece because it was said to strike just as hard.

Gooseberry Lemonade

Summer citrus with tart sweetness. Perfect for outdoor entertaining.

4 gooseberries (sliced in half)
Splash of Simple Syrup (see page 25)
2 ounces chardonnay
4 ounces pink lemonade
Gooseberry (for garnish)

In tall glass, muddle gooseberries and Simple Syrup. Fill glass with crushed ice. Add chardonnay and pink lemonade. Stir until combined well.

Garnish with a gooseberry placed on the lip of the glass.

Plum Sour

Simple ingredients with bold, balanced flavors.

TOOL BOX

▸ Mixing glass
▸ Tin
▸ Strainer
▸ Knife
▸ Muddler

Tall/Collins glass

3 plum wedges

2 ounces Fresh Sour (see page 26)

2 ounces bourbon

Splash of pasteurized egg white (look for small cartons
    of pasteurized egg white in the dairy section)

Peach bitters

In a mixing glass, muddle plums, Fresh Sour, and bourbon until combined well. Add egg white. Add crushed ice to tall glass. Set aside. Add ice to tin and shake cocktail. Strain over crushed ice into tall glass. Top with 3 drops of peach bitters.

In his 1862 book *How to Mix Drinks*, Jerry Thomas describes sours as drinks made with brandy. Today, a sour is a mixed drink with a base spirit, lemon or lime juice, and a sweetener.

Fresh Tomato Bloody Mary

TOOL BOX

- ▶ Mixing glass
- ▶ Tin
- ▶ Strainer
- ▶ Sieve
- ▶ Knife
- ▶ Muddler

Cocktail glass

Ripe summer flavors. Not just for brunch anymore!

6 cherry tomatoes

1 basil leaf

Pinch of fresh oregano

Pinch of salt

Pinch of ground black pepper

Dash of Tabasco sauce

Dash of Worcestershire sauce

Juice of 1 lemon wedge

1½ ounces citrus vodka (may substitute silver tequila)

1 oregano sprig (for garnish)

In mixing glass, muddle 5 tomatoes, basil, oregano, salt, pepper, Tabasco sauce, Worcestershire sauce, and lemon juice. Add citrus vodka. Add ice to tin. Shake well. Double-strain into cocktail glass using the strainer on the shaker while pouring contents through the sieve placed over the glass.

Garnish with an oregano sprig speared through remaining cherry tomato.

The Bloody Mary was created in the 1920s by Fernand "Pete" Petiot, a bartender at Harry's New York Bar in Paris, France. The name stuck because it reminded a patron of a woman named Mary from The Bucket of Blood Club in Chicago. In the 1930s, Petiot unsuccessfully tried to change the name of this famous cocktail to the Red Snapper.

Lychee Madras

Crisp citrus with a nutty sweetness.

TOOL BOX

▶ Blender
▶ Cocktail pick
▶ Straw

Tall/Collins glass

1½ ounces lemon vodka
2 ounces cranberry juice
1 ounce fresh orange juice
Juice of 1 lime wedge
3 lychee nuts

Place one tall glass of ice in blender. Add vodka, cranberry juice, orange juice, lime juice, and 2 lychee nuts. Blend until ice is crushed. Pour into a tall glass.

Garnish with remaining lychee nut on a cocktail pick

Caliente Mango Freeze

Kick up your party with this hot and cool cocktail.
Serve with chips and salsa.

TOOL BOX

▶ Mixing glass
▶ Tin
▶ Strainer
▶ Knife
▶ Muddler
▶ Ice cream scoop
▶ Grater
▶ Sauté pan

Rocks glass

1 mango (cubed)

1 jalapeño pepper (cut into wheels)

¼ cup Simple Syrup (see page 25)

2 scoops lemon sorbet

½ ounce Fresh Sour (see page 26)

2 ounces reposado tequila

Lime zest

Cube mango and slice 2 jalapeño wheels. Add to sauté pan with Simple Syrup. Sauté on medium heat until mango is soft. Cool.

Add lemon sorbet to rocks glass.

In mixing glass, muddle mango compote, Fresh Sour, and tequila. Add ice to tin. Shake well. Strain over sorbet. Zest about ¼ teaspoon of lime over cocktail. Enjoy with a spoon and straw.

Honeydew Sake Cocktail

TOOL BOX

- ▸ Mixing glass
- ▸ Tin
- ▸ Strainer
- ▸ Knife
- ▸ Muddler
- ▸ Citrus press

Cocktail glass

Elevate the subtle flavors of honeydew with lemon grass and sake. Serve with Asian cuisine.

Juice of 1 medium lemon (approximately 1½ ounces)

5 1-inch honeydew cubes

2 ounces sake

½ ounce Lemon Grass Syrup (see page 26)

Small stalk of lemon grass (for garnish)

To mixing glass, add lemon juice and 4 honeydew cubes. Muddle. Add sake and Lemon Grass Syrup. Add ice to tin. Shake well. Strain into cocktail glass.

Garnish with remaining honeydew cube speared with a stalk of lemon grass.

Toasts for Summer

I thank you for your welcome,
Which was cordial,
And your cordial,
Which is welcome.

Nothing but the best for our hostess,
That's why she has us as friends.

May the luck of the Irish possess you,
May the devil fly off with your worries,
And may God bless you forever and ever.
—Irish folklore

Autumn

Abundance. Harvest. Appreciation.

Cozy Pomegranate Cider

Warm up to these rich, fall flavors.

2 cups apple cider
1 cup red wine
½ cup pomegranate juice
2 cinnamon sticks
10-15 whole cloves
4-5 pomegranate seeds (per cocktail, for garnish)

RIM INGREDIENTS
4 bar spoons super fine sugar
¼ bar spoon cinnamon
Lime wedge

TO RIM THE GLASS:

On a small plate, measure sugar and cinnamon. Stir. Rim the outside top of mug with lime wedge. Roll the outside rim of the mug in the sugar mixture. Set aside.

Add apple cider, wine, pomegranate juice, cinnamon sticks, and cloves to a saucepan. Bring to a simmer on low heat.

Strain hot cider through a sieve into sugar-rimmed mug.

Garnish by dropping pomegranate seeds in cider. Seeds will gently float to the bottom of the glass.

Gibson with Homemade Cocktail Onions

TOOL BOX

▶ Mixing glass
▶ Tin
▶ Strainer
▶ Cocktail pick

Cocktail glass

Homemade cocktail onions are perfect in a martini and make a wonderful hostess gift.

Dry vermouth

3 ounces gin

Homemade Cocktail Onions (see recipe on next page)

Rinse the inside of cocktail glass with dry vermouth by swirling vermouth on inside of glass and pouring it out, leaving only residue in the glass.

Add gin to mixing glass. Add ice to tin. Shake well. Strain into seasoned cocktail glass.

Garnish with 2 Homemade Cocktail Onions on a pick.

The Gibson cocktail is named after an American diplomat who served in Europe during Prohibition. He was described as a teetotaller who attended many events where Martinis were served. To avoid drinking, he requested that his glass of water be garnished with an onion, so he could easily distinguish it from the other cocktails.

Homemade Cocktail Onion Recipe

1 pound fresh pearl onions

½ cup cider vinegar

½ cup red wine vinegar

½ cup water

½ cup salt

⅔ cup sugar

1 rosemary sprig

8 juniper berries

12 whole allspice

1 bar spoon chai spice blend

1 bar spoon black pepper

½ bar spoon minced garlic

1 cup bianco vermouth

In a saucepan, add pearl onions and cover with water. Bring to a boil on high heat. Reduce heat and simmer for 10 minutes. Drain water. Cut ends off onions and peel. Place onions in a glass container. Add following ingredients back to the saucepan: cider vinegar, red wine vinegar, water, salt, sugar, rosemary, juniper berries, allspice, chai spice blend, black pepper, and minced garlic.

Let ingredients simmer on low heat for 20 minutes. Strain liquid over onions. Let cool. Add bianco vermouth. Mix together.

Store onions in a sealed container in refrigerator.

The Apple Cocktail

*Dazzle your guests with this Thanksgiving cocktail.
Served in an apple instead of a glass.*

TOOL BOX

- Apple corer
- Mixing glass
- Tin
- Strainer
- Knife
- Muddler

Cored apple

1 whole apple (select one with a flatter bottom)

Juice of 1 lemon wedge

1 apple wedge (cut in half)

1 ounce unsweetened apple juice

1 ounce limoncello

½ ounce vanilla vodka

Splash cranberry juice

1 cinnamon stick (for garnish)

Core the apple to about the halfway point. Be certain not to cut through the bottom. Use the lemon wedge to squeeze a small amount of lemon juice on inside of cored apple. Set aside.

In mixing glass, muddle apple wedge and unsweetened apple juice. Add limoncello, vanilla vodka, and cranberry juice. Shake well. Strain into cored apple and serve with a small straw.

Garnish with a cinnamon stick.

Cinnamon Fig Sidecar

TOOL BOX

▸ Mixing glass
▸ Tin
▸ Strainer
▸ Sieve (optional)
▸ Knife
▸ Bar spoon
▸ Muddler

Cocktail glass

Enjoy the rich, toasty flavors of cognac as it brings out the sweetness of fresh figs.

1 black mission fig
1½ ounces Fresh Sour (see page 26)
Pinch of cinnamon
½ ounce orange curaçao
1½ ounces VSOP cognac

RIM INGREDIENTS
4 bar spoons super fine sugar
Lime wedge

TO RIM THE GLASS:

On a small plate, measure the sugar. Rim the outside top of glass with lime wedge. Roll the outside rim of the glass in the sugar. Set aside.

Remove stem from the fig, cut a thin slice for the garnish, and dice the remainder. Add diced fig and Fresh Sour to mixing glass. Muddle until combined well. Add a small pinch of cinnamon, orange curaçao, and cognac. Add ice to tin. Shake hard. Strain into sugar-rimmed cocktail glass.

Garnish with fig slice.

....

This cocktail was created at Paris's Harry's New York Bar by barman Pete Petiot and named for a World War I American Army captain living in Paris who was driven to the bar each day in a motorcycle sidecar. The original Sidecar is a fine blend of brandy, triple sec, and lemon.

Piña Colada Cocktail

TOOL BOX

► Mixing glass
► Tin
► Strainer
► Citrus press
► Bar spoon

Cocktail glass

Bring a touch of summer to autumn.

1½ ounces coconut rum
2 ounces fresh coconut water
½ ounce fresh pineapple juice
Juice of ½ a pressed lime
Pineapple leaf (for garnish)

RIM INGREDIENTS
2 bar spoons honey
4 bar spoons coconut flakes

To rim the glass: Measure honey on to a small plate. Measure coconut flakes on to a different small plate. First, rotate the rim of the glass in the honey, coating the top outer lip. Next, roll the honey rim onto the coconut so it coats the honey evenly. Set aside.

To mixing glass, add coconut rum, coconut water, pineapple juice, and lime juice. Add ice to tin. Shake well. Strain into coconut-rimmed cocktail glass.

Garnish with a pineapple leaf.

The Piña Colada was first introduced in 1954 by bartender Ramon "Monchito" Marrero at the Caribe Hilton Hotel in Puerto Rico. It is the official beverage of the hotel. There is also a bar in old San Juan that makes a similar claim.

Grape Escape

A playful cocktail reminiscent of grape soda.

9 concord grapes

½ ounce concord grape juice

½ ounce peach schnapps

1 ounce currant vodka

1 ounce Fresh Sour (see page 26)

Club soda

2 frozen concord grapes (for garnish)

In mixing glass, muddle grapes and grape juice. Add peach schnapps, vodka, and Fresh Sour. Add ice to tin. Shake well. Strain into cocktail glass. Top with club soda.

Garnish with two frozen concord grapes on a pick.

Pear Essence Cosmopolitan

Autumn's best inspires new tradition in this classic favorite.

TOOL BOX

▸ Mixing glass
▸ Tin
▸ Muddler
▸ Knife
▸ Strainer
▸ Sieve
▸ Cocktail pick

Cocktail glass

2 anjou pear slices
Juice of ½ a pressed lime
1 ounce cranberry juice
1½ ounces citrus vodka
½ ounce triple sec
3 cranberries (for garnish)

In mixing glass, muddle pear slices, lime juice, and cranberry juice. Add vodka and triple sec. Add ice to tin. Shake well. Double-strain into glass, using the strainer over the shaker while pouring contents through a sieve placed over the glass.

Garnish with 3 cranberries on a cocktail pick.

The Cosmopolitan got its start between 1956 and 1970, when Ocean Spray began to include cocktail recipes on the label of its fruit juice containers. The original version, known as the Harpoon, was made with vodka, cranberry juice, and lime. Later, triple sec was added and the drink was newly dubbed the Cosmopolitan. The drink was popularized in the 1990s by the television series *Sex in the City*.

Refrescante Fennel Cocktail

A great complement to savory or spicy food.

TOOL BOX

▶ Mixing glass
▶ Tin
▶ Strainer
▶ Knife
▶ Muddler

Tall/Collins glass

> Juice of 1 lime wedge
> 10 fennel seeds
> 2 ounces añejo tequila
> 3 ounces fresh orange juice
> Lime wheel (for garnish)

In mixing glass, squeeze juice from lime wedge over fennel seeds and muddle. Add tequila and fresh orange juice. Add ice to tin. Shake well. Fill tall glass with crushed ice. Strain cocktail into glass.

Garnish with a lime wheel.

Persimmon Indian Summer

TOOL BOX

- Mixing glass
- Tin
- Strainer
- Knife
- Muddler

Cocktail glass

A perfect treat after raking leaves or enjoying the crisp autumn air.

4 persimmons (cubed)

1 ounce Fresh Sour (see page 26)

½ ounce pomegranate juice

6 whole cloves

1½ ounces brandy

Orange wedge (for garnish)

In mixing glass, muddle persimmon cubes and Fresh Sour. Add pomegranate juice, 3 cloves, and brandy. Add ice to tin. Shake well. Double-strain into glass using the strainer on the shaker while pouring contents through a sieve placed over the glass.

Garnish with orange wedge decorated with remaining cloves.

Pumpkin Cocktail

Add this to your Halloween or Thanksgiving dessert menu.

TOOL BOX

▸ Mixing glass
▸ Tin
▸ Strainer
▸ Bar spoon
▸ Knife

Cocktail glass

1½ ounces pumpkin liqueur

1 ounce orange vodka

½ ounce half & half

Splash of vanilla syrup (see page 26)

Gooseberry (for garnish)

RIM INGREDIENTS

4 bar spoons super fine sugar

¼ bar spoon ground cinnamon

Lime wedge

TO RIM THE GLASS:

Measure sugar and cinnamon onto a small plate. Rim outside top of glass with lime wedge. Roll the outside rim of glass in sugar mixture. Set aside.

Add pumpkin liqueur, orange vodka, half and half, and vanilla syrup to mixing glass. Add ice to tin. Shake well. Strain into cocktail glass.

Garnish with a gooseberry. Peel back the outer leaves of the berry. Slit the bottom of the berry. Rest on the rim of the glass.

Toasts for Autumn

Here's to our guest—
Don't let him rest.
But keep his elbow bending.
'Tis time to drink—
Full time to think
Tomorrow—when you're mending.

All our guests make us happy,
Some by coming, and others by going.

The ornament of a house
is the guests who frequent it.

Winter

Cozy. Blustery. Reflection.

Caviar Martini

Luxury in every sip.

Splash dry vermouth

3 ounces gin

Caviar (for garnish)

TOOL BOX

▸ Mixing glass

▸ Tin

▸ Strainer

▸ Mother-of-pearl or other fancy spoon

Cocktail glass

Rinse the inside of cocktail glass with vermouth by swirling vermouth on the inside of the glass and pouring it out, leaving only residue in the glass. Add gin to mixing glass and ice to tin. Shake well. Strain into seasoned cocktail glass.

Garnish with caviar on a fancy spoon.

There are many stories surrounding the history of the Martini. The most well-known is that the Martini is a version of the original cocktail known as the Martinez, which consisted of a sweeter gin called "Old Tom," maraschino cherry liqueur, and bitters. The Martinez was served with a lemon twist. This cocktail was named for a customer who drank at the Occidental Hotel in San Francisco every morning before boarding a ferry to Martinez, California. Today's Martinis consist of gin and dry vermouth served with an olive, onion, or lemon twist as a garnish.

1862

Serve before any meal as an aperitif.

1¼ ounce bianco vermouth
¾ ounce orange curaçao
Juice of 1 lemon wedge
¾ ounce Passion Fruit Purée (see page 27)
Splash of spumante sparkling wine
Orange and lemon spirals (see page 27) (for garnish)

To mixing glass, add vermouth, orange curaçao, lemon juice, and Passion Fruit Purée. Add ice to tin. Shake well. Add spumante. Rock contents of shaker gently. Strain into cocktail glass.

Garnish with an orange and lemon spiral.

As a member of the United States Bartenders Guild, Bridget competed in the Bacardi Martini Grand Prix, the most prestigious cocktail competition in the world. Her 1862 took home the silver medal.

Hot Banana Buttered Rum

TOOL BOX

▸ Spoon
▸ Sauté pan
▸ Bar spoon
▸ Knife
▸ Large
  mixing bowl

Coffee mug

Warm the hearts of your guests with these smells and tastes of the holidays.

1 pound unsalted sweet cream butter (room temperature)
1½ bar spoons ground cinnamon
1½ bar spoons Jamaican allspice
5 bar spoons super fine sugar
10-12 whole cloves
3 medium bananas (optional)
1½ ounces aged or spiced rum
Cinnamon stick (for garnish)

Using a spoon, mix butter, cinnamon, allspice, sugar, and cloves together long enough to combine well. Cool in refrigerator for 2 hours.

Banana version: Slice bananas into 1-inch slices. Add bananas and 5 heaping bar spoons of butter mixture to sauté pan. Sauté until bananas are soft. Add back to bowl of butter mixture. Stir well. Cool as directed.

Spirit-free version: Hold the rum.

To a coffee mug, add two heaping bar spoons of butter mixture. Add 1½ ounces of aged rum. Fill mug with hot water. Stir until butter is melted. Garnish with a cinnamon stick.

Savory Avocado Cocktail

TOOL BOX

▸ Mixing glass
▸ Tin
▸ Knife
▸ Muddler
▸ Strainer or small sieve
▸ Bar spoon

Cocktail glass

The avocado adds a creamy twist to the Margarita. Excellent with Mexican and spicy food.

Avocado
5 fresh tarragon leaves
1½ ounces Fresh Sour (see page 26)
Juice of ½ a pressed lime
1½ ounces añejo tequila
½ ounce triple sec
Tarragon sprig (for garnish)

RIM INGREDIENTS
4 bar spoons super fine sugar
1½ bar spoons sea salt
Lime wedge

TO RIM THE GLASS:

On a small plate mix sugar and salt. Rim the outside top of glass with lime wedge. Roll the outside rim of glass in sugar mixture. Set aside.

Peel and cut avocado into one-inch cubes. To mixing glass, add one cube of avocado, 5 tarragon leaves, Fresh Sour, and lime. Muddle until avocado is well mixed. Add tequila and triple sec. Add ice to the tin. Shake all ingredients well. Double-strain into glass, using the strainer on the shaker while pouring contents through a sieve over the glass.

Garnish with a tarragon sprig.

Mary Pickford

TOOL BOX

▸ Mixing glass
▸ Tin
▸ Strainer

Cocktail glass

Tropical flavors come to life with the fruit of the season.

1½ ounces white rum
½ ounce maraschino liqueur
¼ ounce grenadine
2 ounces fresh pineapple juice
Pineapple spear (for garnish)

To mixing glass, add rum, maraschino liqueur, grenadine, and pineapple juice. Add ice to tin. Shake well. Strain into cocktail glass.

Garnish with a pineapple spear.

This cocktail was created in 1920 at the Hotel Nacional de Cuba, Havana. This refreshing cocktail uses native Cuban ingredients and was named after Mary Pickford, the popular star of silent films who was also known as "America's Sweetheart" and "Little Mary."

Tangerine Orange Mule

Bright citrus flavors make this a modern cocktail.

3 tangerine segments (peeled)
Juice of 1 lime wedge
1½ ounces orange vodka
Splash of ginger beer
Lime wheel (for garnish)

In a short glass, muddle tangerine segments and lime juice. Add orange vodka. Fill glass with crushed ice. Top with ginger beer. Stir with bar spoon until well combined.

Garnish with a lime wheel.

The name Moscow Mule refers to the taste of vodka with an added "kick" provided by the rich flavors of ginger beer. The Moscow Mule was a marriage of interests and combined effort of Jack Morgan, the owner of the Cock 'n' Bull Tavern and a producer of ginger beer; John Martin, the president of a spirits company; and Rudolph Kunett, who worked for a division of that same company. The drink was traditionally served in a copper mug.

Kiwi Champagne

A perfect toast to the holidays.

4 slices of peeled kiwi fruit

Juice of 1 lime wedge

1 sugar cube

4 ounces prosecco sparkling wine

Orange bitters

In mixing glass, muddle kiwi, lime juice, and sugar cube. Add prosecco. Add ice to tin. Rock contents of shaker gently. Strain into flute. Shake two drops of orange bitters on top of cocktail.

TOOL BOX

▸ Knife

▸ Mixing glass

▸ Tin

▸ Strainer

▸ Muddler

Champagne flute

Red Grapefruit Brown Derby

TOOL BOX

▸ Bar spoon
▸ Muddler
▸ Knife
Rocks glass

This herbaceous, sweet version of the Brown Derby is meant to be sipped slowly and enjoyed with friends.

4 small red grapefruit wedges (peel removed)
1 ounce Honey Rosemary Syrup (see page 26)
2 ounces rye whiskey
1 rosemary sprig (for garnish)

In rocks glass, muddle grapefruit and Honey Rosemary Syrup until combined well. Add rye whiskey. Fill to the top with crushed ice. Stir with bar spoon.

Garnish with rosemary sprig.

The Brown Derby was created in the 1930s at California's Vendome Club and named in honor of Wilshire Boulevard's Brown Derby restaurant.

Tall Meyer Lemon Southside

TOOL BOX

▸ Mixing glass
▸ Tin
▸ Strainer
▸ Citrus press
▸ Knife

Tall/Collins glass

A friendly crowd-pleaser, just right for entertaining.

> 2 ounces gin
> 2 ounces juice from meyer lemons
> (approximately 2 lemons)
> 1 ounce Honey Syrup (see page 25)
> 10 mint leaves
> Splash of pasteurized egg white (optional) (look for small
> cartons of pasteurized egg white in the dairy section)
> Club soda
> Lemon wheel (for garnish)

To mixing glass, add gin, lemon juice, Honey Syrup, mint leaves, and egg white. Add ice to tin and to tall glass. Set glass aside. Shake well. Strain into tall glass. Top with club soda.

Garnish with lemon wheel.

....

Although the Southside has a few stories surrounding its origin, one classic favorite is that it was developed during Prohibition by a south-side Chicago gang leader who used sugar and lemon to mask the flavor of bootleg gin. The 21 Club in New York also claims that it is the home of this deliciously refreshing cocktail.

Blood Orange Rickey

TOOL BOX

- ▸ Mixing glass
- ▸ Tin
- ▸ Strainer
- ▸ Citrus press

Tall/Collins glass

As crisp and colorful as a winter sunset.

> 1½ ounces gin
> Juice of 1 pressed blood orange
>   (approximately 2 ounces)
> Juice of ½ a pressed lime
> Club soda
> Blood orange slice (for garnish)

To mixing glass, add gin, blood orange juice, and lime juice. Add ice to tin. Shake well. Strain into ice-filled tall glass. Top with club soda.

Garnish with a blood orange slice.

On an extremely hot, muggy day in 1890, a barman at the Washington, DC bar Shoemaker's made a new drink by simply squeezing lime into a glass of gin and adding soda from a siphon. Colonel Rickey, an English officer and lobbyist, was the first patron to try it; he enjoyed it so much, he asked for seconds. The barman named the drink the Gin Rickey, and its ingredients remain gin, fresh lime, and soda to this day.

Toasts for Winter

May you have the hindsight to know where you've been,
The foresight to know where you're going,
And the insight to know when you're going too far.

May you look back on the past with as much
Pleasure as you look forward to the future.

May we all be alive this time in twelve months.

To champagne,
The drink that makes you see double,
And feel single.

Infusions

Infusions marry your favorite spirit with a season's freshest fruits, produce, herbs, and spices. The combinations are limitless since infusions can be enjoyed just as they are, or used as the base spirit in a creative cocktail, this chapter includes flavorful combinations and cocktail recipes for each infusion.

MAKING YOUR INFUSION

Each market-fresh infusion recipe should be made in a three-quart jar. Remember, the container must be washed and rinsed well, have a lid, and, most importantly, be made of glass. Never attempt to make an infusion in a plastic bottle.

Depending on the ripeness of the fruit, each recipe might produce a larger quantity than can fit back into the original liquor bottle. It's a good idea to have additional clean bottles on hand to accommodate any extra amounts. Always choose the freshest produce, and wash it thoroughly. Always plan ahead: Some infusions can take up to two weeks to be ready. As you will find, they are worth the wait.

(LEFT) Strawberry-Rosemary Infusion (see page 105)

Spring Infusions

Strawberry-Rosemary Infusion

Flavors of the vine right into your glass.

10 pints of sliced strawberries
7 rosemary sprigs
2 750 ml gin

Place strawberries and rosemary in 3-quart glass infusion jar. Pour gin over the fruit. Save original gin bottles. Let rest for 7 days at room temperature. Using a funnel and sieve, strain liquid back into empty liquor bottles. Refrigerate.

Red Martini

3 ounces Strawberry-Rosemary Infusion
Dash of Simple Syrup (see page 25)

Add infusion to mixing glass. Add Simple Syrup to taste. Add ice to tin. Shake well. Strain into a cocktail glass. Garnish with a rosemary sprig.

Salty Puppy Cocktail

2 ounces Strawberry-Rosemary Infusion
3 ounces pink grapefruit juice

RIM INGREDIENTS
Lime wedge
2 bar spoons sea salt

To rim the glass: Measure salt onto a small plate. Rim the outside top of the glass with a lime wedge. Roll the outside rim of the glass in the salt. Set aside.

Add ice to short glass. Pour in infusion and pink grapefruit juice. Stir.

Cucumber Papaya Infusion

Crisp refreshment on a hot summer day.

> 5 English cucumbers (thinly sliced)
> 2 whole papayas (peeled and cubed)
> 2 750 ml gin

Layer fruit into 3-quart glass infusion jar. Add gin. Save liquor bottles. Let rest for 7 days at room temperature. Using a funnel and sieve, strain liquid back into bottles. Refrigerate.

Spa Cocktail

> 3 ounces Cucumber Papaya Infusion
> ½ ounce Fresh Sour (see page 26)
> Cucumber slice (for garnish)

To mixing glass, add infusion and Fresh Sour. Add ice to tin. Shake well. Strain into a cocktail glass.

Garnish with a cucumber slice.

Tea for Two Cocktail

This cocktail is made in a pitcher and meant to be shared.

> 6 ounces Cucumber Papaya Infusion
> 2 ounces Lemon Grass Syrup (see page 26)
> 12 ounces sweetened iced tea flavored with lemon
> Lemon wheels (for garnish)

Add infusion, tea, and Lemon Grass Syrup to a pitcher. Stir. Add ice to tall glasses.

Garnish with a lemon wheel and serve.

Summer Infusions

Bing Cherry Infusion

Balanced nuttiness, blended with tart sweetness.

> 9 pints pitted bing cherries
> 4 cinnamon sticks
> 1 750 ml amaretto
> 1 750 ml VS cognac

Place fruit and cinnamon sticks in infusion jar. Pour amaretto and cognac over the top. Save the empty liquor bottles. Let infusion rest for 14 days at room temperature. Using a funnel and a sieve, strain liquid back into bottles. Place cherries in sealed glass jar and refrigerate them for later use as garnishes on cocktails like the Old Fashioned and Manhattan.

Pirate Berries Infusion

Liven up your rum with rich berries.

> 3 pints blueberries
> 3 pints blackberries
> 3 pints raspberries
> 2 750 ml dark rum
> ½ cup Cinnamon Syrup (see page 25)

Layer berries into infusion jar. Add rum and Cinnamon Syrup. Save original liquor bottles. Let rest at room temperature for 14 days. Using a funnel and sieve, strain liquid into the original bottles. Refrigerate.

Pirate Cocktail

> 3 ounces Pirate Berries Infusion

Add infusion to mixing glass. Add ice to tin. Shake well. Strain into cocktail glass. Garnish with raspberries on a pick.

Pirate's Life Lemonade

> 3 ounces Pirate Berries Infusion
> 4 ounces lemonade
> Lemon wheel (for garnish)

Fill tall glass with ice. Add infusion and lemonade. Stir well.

Garnish with a lemon wheel.

Autumn Infusions

Savory Onion Infusion

I often use Savory Onion Infusion as a marinade for meat or a spicy addition to vodka sauce. Simply add steaks or chicken fillets to a plastic bag and cover with this infusion. Let rest overnight in refrigerator. For a savory kick, substitute this infusion instead of vodka in any vodka sauce recipe.

> 4 large sweet onions (sliced)
> 1 jalapeño pepper (sliced thin)
> 2 green bell peppers (sliced thin)
> 20 peppercorns
> 2 750 ml vodka

Layer onions, jalapeño, bell pepper and peppercorns into 3-quart glass infusion jar. Pour vodka over top. Save the liquor bottles. Let rest for 7 days at room temperature. Using a funnel and sieve, strain back into vodka bottles. Refrigerate.

Spiced Caesar

> 2 ounces Savory Onion Infusion
> 3 ounces Clamato juice
> Clam (for garnish)

Fill tall glass with ice. Add infusion and juice. Stir.

Garnish with a fresh clam.

Fig and Pear Infusion

Combines the warm flavors and spices of the season.

> 4 pounds d'anjou pears (thinly sliced)
> 3 pints figs (cut in half, with stems removed)
> 4 cinnamon sticks
> 10 whole cloves
> 2 bar spoons pumpkin pie spice
> 1 750 ml vodka
> 1 750 ml orange liqueur

Place figs and pear slices in alternate layers in 3-quart glass infusion jar. Add cinnamon sticks, cloves and pumpkin pie spice. Pour vodka and orange liqueur over top. Save the liquor bottles. Let rest for 12 days at room temperature. Using a sieve and funnel, strain back into original bottles. Store in refrigerator.

Harvest Time

2 ounces Fig & Pear Infusion
½ ounce fresh orange juice
½ ounce Fresh Sour

RIM INGREDIENTS
4 bar spoons super fine sugar
¼ bar spoon cinnamon
Lime wedge
Pear slice (for garnish) (Use juice of lemon wedge on pear slice
    to prevent it from turning brown or oxidizing)

To rim the glass: On a small plate, combine sugar and cinnamon.
Rim the outside top of the glass with lime wedge. Roll the outside rim
of the cocktail glass in sugar mixture. Set aside.

Add infusion, juice, and Fresh Sour to mixing glass. Add ice to tin.
Shake well. Strain into sugar-cinnamon rimmed cocktail glass.

Garnish with a pear slice.

Fall Fizz

2 ounces Fig and Pear Infusion
Splash of egg white (optional) (look for small
    cartons of pasteurized egg white in the dairy section)
2 ounces Fresh Sour (see page 26)
1 ounce ginger ale
Cinnamon stick (for garnish)

To mixing glass, add infusion, egg white, and Fresh Sour. Add ice to
tin. Shake well. Strain into ice-filled tall glass. Top with ginger ale.

Garnish with a cinnamon stick.

Winter Infusions

Pineapple-Blood Orange Infusion

Bring home these tropical flavors to chase away the winter blues.

> 3 pounds blood oranges (peeled and sliced into wedges)
> 2 whole pineapples (peeled and cubed)
> 10 mint sprigs
> 2 750 ml vodka

Layer fruit and mint into 3-quart glass infusion jar. Save pineapple leaves. Add vodka. Save liquor bottles. Let rest for 7 days at room temperature. Using a funnel and sieve, strain back into vodka bottles. Store in refrigerator.

Snow Day

> 4 ounces Pineapple-Blood Orange Infusion (see above)
> Crushed ice or fresh snow
> Pineapple leaf (for garnish)

Fill short glass with crushed ice or snow. Add infusion directly from chilled bottle.

Garnish with a pineapple leaf.

Long Weekend

> 2 ounces Pineapple-Blood Orange Infusion
> ½ ounce passion fruit juice
> ½ ounce Fresh Sour (see page 26)
> Rosé Champagne

In mixing glass, add infusion, passion fruit juice, and Fresh Sour. Add ice to tin. Shake well. Strain into a champagne flute. Top with rosé champagne.

Kiwi-Tangerine Infusion

Bright flavors with the warmth of rum.

> 5 pounds kiwi (peeled and sliced)
> 2 pounds tangerines (peeled and sliced into wedges)
> 2 750 ml white rum

Layer fruit into 3-quart glass infusion jar. Add rum. Save liquor bottles. Let rest at room temperature for 7 days. Using a funnel and sieve, strain into original bottles. Store in refrigerator.

Jack Frost

> 2 ounces Kiwi-Tangerine Infusion
> ½ ounce Rosemary Honey Syrup (see page 26)
> 2 ounces apple juice
> Juice of 1 lime wedge
> Kiwi slice (for garnish)

To mixing glass, add infusion, Rosemary Honey Syrup, apple juice, and juice of a lime wedge. Add ice to tin. Shake well. Strain into an ice-filled short glass.

Garnish with a kiwi wheel.

Monday, Monday

> 3 ounces Kiwi-Tangerine Infusion
> Tangerine wedge (for garnish)

Add infusion to mixing glass. Add ice to tin. Shake well. Strain into an ice-filled short glass.

Garnish with a tangerine wedge.

Tilly's Limoncello Infusion

In honor of Great-Great Aunt Tilly, pictured at right. Aunt Tilly was the first female bartender in my family. She was a stunning woman with lavender eyes who was as sturdy as she was beautiful. She managed the family tavern in the coal-mining town of Coal City, Illinois, during an era when women were not allowed to be patrons. This infusion is dedicated to the courageous spirit of women and celebrates Tilly's Italian heritage.

Rinds of 9 large lemons
Rinds of 4 large oranges
2 vanilla beans (sliced lengthwise)
1 750 ml vodka
1 cup Simple Syrup
½ bar spoon cream of tartar

Add fruit rinds to 3-quart glass infusion jar. Add vanilla and pour vodka over the top. Save liquor bottle. Let rest for 3 weeks in a dark, cool location. Using a sieve and funnel, strain into original vodka bottle. Add Simple Syrup and cream of tartar. Mix well. Refrigerate.

Index